Should We Get Married?

How to Evaluate Your Relationship

William P. Smith

New
Growth
Press

www.newgrowthpress.com

New Growth Press, Greensboro, NC 27429
Copyright © 2008 by Christian Counseling & Educational Foundation. All rights reserved. Published 2008

Cover Design: The DesignWorks Group, Nate Salciccioli and Jeff Miller, www.thedesignworksgroup.com

Typesetting: Robin Black, www.blackbirdcreative.biz

ISBN-10: 1-934885-33-9
ISBN-13: 978-1-934885-33-8

Library of Congress Cataloging-in-Publication Data

Smith, William P., 1965-
  Should we get married? : how to evaluate your relationship / William P. Smith.
     p. cm.
  Includes bibliographical references and index.
  ISBN 978-1-934885-33-8
  1. Marriage—Religious aspects—Christianity. 2. Marriage counseling. I. Title.
  BV835.S69 2008
  248.4—dc22

                                        2008011926

Printed in Canada
10 11 12   6 5 4

FSC
Mixed Sources
Cert no. SW-COC-000952
© 1996 FSC

Alex and Melissa smiled at me and asked, "How does premarital counseling work? When will you tell us that it's okay for us to get married?"

I smiled back and answered, "Never."

I knew they were puzzled, so I explained, "It would be impossible for me, after talking with you for only a few hours, to know enough about you to say, 'I think you should get married.' So what can I do? I can help you think about how to strengthen your relationship, so you will have the foundation for a good marriage. I can help you work on parts of your relationship that are weak. And I can alert you to issues that are potentially dangerous or destructive. I'll be glad to give you a yellow light to slow down or a red light to stop, but I'll never give you a green light to go ahead. That final light is between you and God, as you assess your relationship."

Although you aren't sitting down with me for face-to-face premarital counseling like Alex and Melissa, we can still evaluate your relationship together. Use this article to assess your relationship in the different areas discussed. If your relationship is weak in one or more of them, then that's a yellow light: Slow your relationship down and work on strengthening it. If you see patterns that are the opposite of what they should be, then that's a red light, and you should seriously question the health of your relationship. You shouldn't consider marriage until those patterns are reversed.

On the other hand, if your relationship is growing in each area, then keep moving forward. Don't look for perfection—even the best human relationships are marred by sin and need to grow in maturity. But you should be able to list concrete examples that show how your relationship has grown in each area.

Share a Common Vision

It's crucial that you share a common vision. Are you both followers of Jesus Christ? Are you both committed to living for him? If you don't share a mutual love for Jesus, you will be pulled in opposite directions at the most important, foundational level of your lives. This will keep you from true intimacy with your partner, threaten the long-term stability of your relationship, and tempt you to compromise your faith (Mark 3:25; 2 Corinthians 6:14).

If you are both followers of Jesus and share a common vision, how do your love for Jesus and your desire to follow him express itself in your relationship on a day-to-day basis?

- Do you appeal to the Bible for help when you have conflicts or confusing decisions to make?
- Is God involved in your relationship? Do his thoughts, values, goals, and attitudes shape you on a daily basis?
- Do you pray together?
- Do you share what God is teaching you from his Word with each other?

- When was the last time God's plans, purposes, and concerns made a difference to what you thought, said, or did as a couple?

With Jesus as your foundation, consider to what extent your dreams for the future are shared.

- Are your desires for lifestyle, family size, occupation, and geographical location similar?
- If you started with different goals in any of these areas, are you able to work toward agreement?

Another way to tell if your relationship is centered on Jesus is by how you (as a couple) deal with difficulties.

- Do you point each other to Christ as you experience problems?
- When you're struggling with feeling anxious, angry, discouraged, confused, or overwhelmed, does your partner listen well

and help you see how Jesus meets the need you have?

- Do you respond well when you are pointed to Christ?

Track Record of Handling Conflicts

When Tom and Nancy proudly told me that in ten years of marriage they had never had a fight, I cringed. How can two sinners completely mesh their lives and not have a conflict or disagreement? They can't. Tom and Nancy avoided conflict by ignoring problems in their relationship. They threw themselves into their careers, took trips, and had fun...until the baby came. Life wasn't fun or glamorous anymore, and their marriage crumbled.

They hadn't learned how to handle conflict and grow under the pressures that produce conflict. They wasted the time before their marriage and their first ten years of married life by not addressing the conflicts that came with the pressures in their lives.

Pressure often builds to explosive strength around the common marital flashpoints of money, sex, and children.

Your relationship faces these same pressures now, but you experience them in different ways because you're not married yet. Learning to deal with pressure before you get married will give you a foundation for handling them within marriage. Now is the time to learn when to speak the truth in love (Ephesians 4:15), when to overlook a fault (Proverbs 19:11), and when to submit to one another in love (Ephesians 5:21).

How do you handle money? Every family has a limited amount of resources—time, money, space, etc. As a single person you are relatively free to spend each in the way you choose, but as a couple you have to work together to decide how to use the finite quantity of the time, money, and space that God has given you. Making those decisions exposes the values and goals of you and your partner. As you might have already noticed, sometimes you disagree.

The way you handle such agenda clashes now—compromise, manipulate, whine, give in—is the way you'll handle them later.

- Do you sense a mutual concern for each other's interests in your present sharing of resources as you plan activities, decide whose parents and friends to visit, and what to do with your "downtime"?
- Do you both look to the other's interests? Or only to your own? (Philippians 2:4)

Think about potential trouble spots in the future by noticing differences in the ways you go about acquiring things. Look around at the things your friend surrounds himself with—his furniture, tools, kitchen appliances, car, electronics, etc.

- Does he always want the best?
- Make do with what he has?
- Does he not really care at all?

• Do you approach material things in the same way or differently?

How do you handle sex? Sex within marriage is a very vivid marker that lets you see the quality of your care for each other. Healthy couples mutually concern themselves with each other's comfort—sleep, relaxation, healthy eating, and exercise—without wrongly indulging each other.

The opposite of mutual concern is taking advantage of each other. One or both of you may ask for too much from the other, give too little, or oddly enough, give too much (and allow the other person to mistakenly believe it's okay to live for his own pleasure).

Before you are married, it's easy to think that you have fulfilled your responsibility to care for your partner if you avoid sexual intimacy. This is an important and necessary way for you to care for one another now. Please realize, however, that caring for one another goes far beyond not sinning sexually with your partner. The opposite of taking advantage of each other is not only restraint, but active concern for the other's best physical interests.

- Do you end a date when you see he's tired and needs to sleep, but neither of you wants to go home?
- Does it matter to you that she regularly dines on popcorn and brownies after work?
- Are you willing to make an issue of his unwillingness to get an annual physical?
- Do you plan dates that tempt both of you physically?

How do you handle children? Children introduce new dynamics into a relationship. They require you to work together, to give up your own desires, and to serve in new ways. But serving other people should not be a new element of your relationship. Serving should already characterize your relationship with each other. Remember, Jesus did not come to be served, but to serve and give his life for us (Matthew 20:28). Jesus calls us to follow in his steps and express our faith in love and service (Galatians 5:13).

Assess whether or not you lay down your own interests to serve each other.

- With what attitudes do you serve?
- Do you serve joyfully, quickly, and thankfully?
- Or do you complain and serve grudgingly, slowly, or not at all?
- Where, as a couple, do you give to others? Dangers can come from too much serving as well as too little.
- Does giving to others substitute for knowing each other?
- Does your giving come from joy or duty?
- Do you give only as a way to feel good about yourself?

We have gone through a lot of tough questions in a short period of time. Don't be overwhelmed. Instead, take the time now to go through these questions slowly and thoughtfully, and don't do it alone. Ask the person you are thinking about marrying to go through the questions with you.

Practical Strategies for Change

Asking hard, honest questions about your relationship is not easy, but your willingness to do so shows your maturity. This will help you to honestly assess your relationship and decide what to do next. Use the exercises below to diagnose the strengths and weaknesses of your current relationship.

1. *Answer the bulleted questions in the first part of this booklet.* Write down your answers, and make sure you include examples from the past two weeks that support your answers. You and your friend should both do this, but not together! Work on the questions separately and then share your answers with each other when you are finished.

2. *Compare your list with your friend's list.* Are you in agreement? Does one of you argue or lobby for his view? Does either of you retreat? You will have a lot to talk about as you go through your answers together.

3. *Assess your lists together.* Are there positive reasons for moving your relationship forward? Can you see weaknesses in your relationship that mean you need to slow down? Are there negative patterns that need to change before you even consider deepening your relationship? What do you think: green, yellow, or red?

Your answers will help you and your friend decide whether you need to slam on the brakes, slow down and grow more, or seriously consider marriage.

Handling Input from Family and Friends

As you work to assess your relationship, you might have noticed already that your family and friends have also assessed your relationship and have strong opinions too. What place should their input have in your decision to get married? And how should you handle their input?

Families and friends often know us better than we know ourselves. So we grow in our understanding of ourselves by having other people—divine as well as human—tell us what they experience of us. That can be very valuable when you are making a big decision like marriage.

For example, I counseled a young couple, Seong and Grace. They had an advantage over many of their peers. Their families were actively involved in their decision to get married without being intrusive or controlling. Both families met and talked together before the two considered engagement since, in their culture, marriage means that the family-groups are joining each other. Both families left the decision to their children, but they met to make sure there were no glaring issues the younger generation had missed.

Their help was a blessing to Seong and Grace. But what is meant to be a blessing can also be a curse in a fallen world. Families can be too intrusive, as well as too passive. Sometimes they push their own agenda; sometimes they try to live out their own desires through our decisions. A healthy balance is needed: You need input from others, and you need to realize that ultimately you will answer to Jesus for what you did with other people's input. You will not answer directly to them.

If you find yourself falling off the horse on either side—valuing other's advice too strongly, or not caring about it enough—then ask God to help you consider what others say, and also know that your decision is yours alone as you stand before Jesus. In the Bible, we are given wonderful direction on this issue. God said in Genesis, "For this reason a man will leave his father and mother and be united to his wife, and they will become one flesh" (Genesis 2:24). This was said in the context of a culture that placed a high value on the role the family played in an individual's life. Until you are ready to leave your family of origin and create a new family unit, you are not ready to get engaged. Creating a new family unit doesn't necessarily mean you leave your family physically, but it does mean that your first priority becomes your new family. Your decisions should reflect that new priority.

What to Do About "Cold Feet"

Perhaps you are already engaged, but you are questioning whether or not you really should get married. How can you decide if you really should slow down your relationship, or if your problem is that you are afraid to get married?

Getting "cold feet" during your engagement is normal—you're making a make huge, life-altering decision! But if you're being treated in a way that concerns you or if your feelings are completely unsettled, then you should seriously consider if committing yourself to this person is a good idea. You should be even more concerned if your fiancé or fiancée dismisses your concerns.

Often when people are engaged and want to slow down or break the engagement, they don't because they're afraid. Here are some things you might be thinking:

- I committed myself already by saying "yes" when he proposed, so that means there's no going back.
- What will mom (or dad, friends, your relatives, his relatives) think if I break off the engagement?
- We've gone so far. Breaking things off now would be so hurtful to her (and everybody else).
- It's too late now. I just have to go through with this and hope for the best.

Engagement in the United States is very, very serious…but it is not binding. You have the freedom to call off the wedding all the way up to "I do." No one else will have to live with the person you marry except you (and your children should you have them), so this is your decision.

There will be consequences to breaking off your engagement. You may have to pay for some or all of the wedding preparations, and some of your relationships may be strained, but that's a lot less costly than being married to someone you shouldn't have.

Begin by asking your fiancé if you could postpone your wedding day. His or her reaction will help you. If she tries to win you to her way of seeing things rather than caring for the way you feel, or he aggressively pushes against your request, then you're probably right to have questions.

Such questions should not remain yours alone. God saves us individually (Ephesians 2:1–10), but he saves us into a community (Ephesians 2:11–22) in part to help us grow up and mature (Ephesians 4:13–16). Make use of your Christian community. Reach out to your family of course, but make sure you get the advice of those God has put around you to help you (pastors, elders, deacons, mentors, wiser older couples, etc.).

Look at the Foundation of Your Relationship

Answering the questions in this article should help you decide whether or not your relationship is built on a solid foundation. Sadly many relationships are built upon poor foundations. Often people develop a serious relationship or even marry simply to meet their own needs. In a healthy relationship, when one person is weak the other person helps (Ecclesiastes 4:9–10). But a healthy relationship is not defined by one person's weaknesses.

If you find that you are regularly making allowances for another's relational failings—to others or even to yourself—then your relationship is unbalanced. Helping a person grow is good. Helping a person stay weak or immature is bad. Is your relationship mutually interdependent or is one person regularly adjusting for the other?

As you work through different issues in your

relationship, pray for wisdom to know whether or not your relationship should slow down or go forward. Remember you are not looking for a perfect relationship or a perfect partner, but for someone who is growing in love for God, you, and other people. As you depend on God for wisdom, he will help you decide whether your relationship should move toward marriage.

If you were encouraged by reading this booklet, perhaps you or someone you know would also be blessed from these booklets: